Zahra M.M.A. Sadiq

The Gifted Individual and
the Right to Education

Author Zahra M.M.A. Sadiq

Cover-design Zahra M.M.A. Sadiq

Layout and typesetting Zahra M.M.A. Sadiq

© 2016 Zahra M.M.A. Sadiq

One of the greatest gifts is the ability to choose an extraordinary example and to invest effort in an achievement, thereby becoming a model oneself

The right to education of the gifted child or adult person has to take into account the specific pedagogical requirements the person's aptitude demands. The term giftedness is open to interpretation and often equated with an expected behaviour considered to prove advanced learning ability in comparison to other students. It is also assumed that this behaviour can be explored using IQ tests or grades. Intellectual ability consists of a variety of coherent skills including literature, logic, music, law, the natural sciences and other realms of scholarship. The basis for a right to education of the capable individual is the developmental support of the complex nature of the human mind and innate capacity with adequate measures.

Giftedness

The development of the criteria of the gifted individual's right to education can be studied from different points of view, such as psychology, education, neurology, philosophy, religion and the social and legal sciences. Thus a multidisciplinary and interdisciplinary approach to this subject is required.

While psychometricians assume that it is possible to measure the structure of high ability by judging the performance on an IQ or EQ test or comparable tests, the proponents of the complex nature of intelligence point out the limited suitability of such tests for revealing the nature of exceptional skill. The didactic reduction applied in the framework of examinations at schools or universities or IQ or comparable tests has not been proven suitable for individuals possessing the ability to cope with complex knowledge.[1]

The support for individuals with exceptional skills serves to enable the gifted person to develop and maintain his personality as a complex character with a gift and thus to facilitate the framing of a sound self-perception and the safeguarding of the peculiar traits as an exceptionally skilled student, artist or scientist. The circumstantial aspects of identity include those traits which are inescapable such as giftedness. Defining his talent as a principal peculiarity of character is fundamental in the gifted individual's responsibility for the

---

1 Gardner, Howard, Frames of Mind. The Theory of Multiple Intelligences, New York 2011, xxix.

development of his self-identity. If the person rejects these characteristics which are essential for his sound self-image, he feels alienated from them. [2] The gift is characterized by specific extraordinary abilities forming the individual talent as a specific trait of unique personality. The social development of the gifted individual is partially dependent on labels based on the judgement of relatives, politicians, journalists, teachers, lawyers, social scientists and psychologists, which can be realistic or erroneous. The bright person has to be enabled early on to recognize his social context, to discover his position in it and to adapt to his environment, bringing it into a balance with his self-concept in order to develop the ability to pursue goal-directed activity. [3]

The talented individual possesses the ability to produce an output without adequate input and does not necessarily need a special education in order to realize

---

2 Oshana, Marina A. L., Autonomy and Self-Identity, in: Autonomy and the Challenges to Liberalism. New Essays, Cambridge 2008, 77-97, 81-86.
3 Gowan, John Curtis, Alienation, in: California Personnel and Guidance Association, Vol. 1, 1968-69, 4-7.

his potential and to adapt to the learning environment when necessary. Even if he is subject to an inadequate education he has the ability for realistic and artistic thinking, wisdom and reasoning, creating and developing, versatility and expertise, and he is capable of inquiry and creating extraordinary achievements. According to persons of average intelligence, the gifted individual is able to take responsibility for his actions. While a student of average aptitude can achieve an advanced output when he is adequately instructed by an excellent teacher, talent frequently causes the bright individual to search for possibilities to realize his potential and to create the way while using it. Since the gifted person possesses the ability to develop a conception of knowledge and to study in the form of self-educated reflection and production, education should refrain from suppressing these traits by measures or activities restricting the individual's learning, drafting and experience given that it is better to align the scale to the skill rather than the skill to the scale. Giftedness is subject to a dynamic directed towards self-preservation which is not an attribute of the ability to lead but to create. Ingeniously talented experts challenge their

4

teachers, evading direct confrontation and raising their objections originating works and introducing new standards in science or art.[4]

Bright individuals who are qualified should contribute to "the objective of intellectuals in a society" which "is to ensure the values of ethics[5] and reason in addition to autonomy, self-perfection and authenticity by acting in terms of publications, teaching or forms of academic professions independent from direct political influence.[6] Appreciating excellent scientists and artists offers the chance for society to benefit from their activity. The capacity of an individual with high ability to exert influence in public depends on a variety of circumstances

---

4 Gardner, Howard, Intelligenzen. Vielfalt des menschlichen Geistes, fourth ed., Stuttgart 2013, 159.
5 The capacity to understand the intricate law of ethics is based on the following statements taken from the Noble Quran: the sura The Heights: (179) {They have hearts with which they do not understand} and the sura Muhammad: (24) {Then do they not reflect upon the Quran, or are there locks upon [their] hearts?}, Abd al-Aziz, Amir, Huquq al-insan fi-l-islam, 1997, 162.
6 Baumann, Zygmunt, Legislators and Interpreters. On Modernity, Post-Modernity and Intellectuals, Cambridge et al. 1995, 191-198.

affecting the reception of the extraordinary oeuvre and its communication. Since society is based on traditions, a person rebuilding a significant theory or establishing a new standard by creating a new genre or excelling in the framework of an existing field will not infrequently meet resistance. The oeuvre of the artist or scientist who possesses the ability to initiate lasting changes, considerably affecting his specific domain, will be appreciated in case it is in the interests of the environment, and his significance can only be assessed posthumously.

Scope of the right to education

The psychological term giftedness is based on a scientific approach which takes into account sociological and biological methods. It is the basis for a policy defining the role of the individual in his educational and professional environment in terms of the constitution and laws. The political implementation of the concept of giftedness, which has to consider the legal basis arising from the rule of law, is a form of practical application which does not coincide with scientific theory. In the legal realm, the lawgiver and the judge have to respect the psychological findings. The transfer of theories of talent into the science of law can take the form of general codifications or detailed regulations. In both cases the lawgiver and the judge have scope for interpretation.

Since schooling plays a key role in life and in the system of economic, social and cultural rights, the right to education of the gifted individual is ruled in international and regional treaties and the constitutions of many countries. The content of the right to education ruled in international and regional treaties should be interpreted as a general provision offering a variety of possibilities for each culture to determine their laws according to the advantage of the specific and dynamic circumstances of the country and culture concerned.

There is no rule determining the age education has to start and the end for compulsory education, which is not synonymous with compulsory school attendance, since some countries permit education to take place outside of school, for example via home schooling. Relevant to all levels of education from primary to higher education are the aspects of availability, accessibility, acceptability and adaptability.[7] Appropriate measures including education free of charge or the introduction of scholarships and other forms of financial support facilitate economic accessibility.[8]

The right to education of the capable person comprises the development of skills according to his merit in order to prevent him from being forced to keep the effect of his talent in form of his oeuvre secret.

---

[7] UN Committee on ESC Rights, General Comment No. 13, UN Doc. E/1999/10.
[8] Verheyde, Mieke, Article 28. The Right to Education. A Commentary on the United Nations Convention on the Rights of the Child, ed. by Alen, André, Vande Lanotte, Johan et al., Leiden et al. 2006, 13, 15 und 24.

Education serves to enable the person to lead a life according to his merit, achievements and concepts.

Article XII of the American Declaration of the Rights and Duties of Man, Likewise every person has the right to an education that will prepare him to attain a decent life, to raise his standard of living, (...).

Extraordinary contributions should be judged subject to the involvement of skilled and gifted scientists and artists and appreciated with appropriate scholarships corresponding to the common procedure of sponsoring the achievements of nongifted persons.

Legal realisations

The schooling of gifted students is subject to legal and executive acts and the right to education is legally enforceable in case a substantial and procedural right exists. It is realized at the international and regional level in the form of contracts and ruled by national constitutions and laws. Merit or capacity is assumed in case the student shows learning behaviour considered to prove his advanced study skills in comparison to other students.

In order to enforce the right to education, the individual has the possibility to take legal action and use the national administrative and judicial procedures which may be consistent with the rules of the International Covenant in Economic, Social and Cultural Rights.

In theory, the negatively phrased right of defence includes the right of the gifted person to oblige the state to refrain from interventions which could impede the development of his potential. The right of participation presupposes the involvement of gifted individuals from all age groups in appropriate educational and cultural programs according to their capacity during each phase of their schooling and professional life on equal terms

10

with persons of average mental condition. The performance right implies that the gifted person has the right to receive special sponsoring for extraordinary achievements in each phase of life to the same extend as individuals of regular aptitude. The premises and scope of the right to protection reserved for three-pole relationships are debatable.[9]

---

9 Schliesky, Utz, Hoffmann, Christian et al., Schutzpflichten und Drittwirkung im Internet. Das Grundgesetz im digitalen Zeitalter, ed. by the Deutsches Institut für Vertrauen und Sicherheit im Internet, Vol. 1, Baden-Baden 2014, 47.

International

In contrast to Article 2 of the International Covenant on Civil and Political Rights, the International Covenant on Economic, Social and Cultural Rights does not rule the justiciability of the ESC rights. In case these are violated it is possible to derive the obligation by means of extending Article 2 section 1.[10] Martin Kriele advocates the dualism of civil and political rights which are directly applicable by the courts and economic, social and cultural rights presupposing the implementation by the legislative corresponding to the cultural and religious preconditions of the country. [11] The infringement of economic, social and cultural rights is often the presupposition for the violation of civil and political rights based on the social and economic order of the state. The justiciability and enforceability of the international right to

---

[10]Agreeing to the result Beiter, Klaus Dieter, The Protection of the Right to Education by International Law. Including a Systematic Analysis of Article 13 of the International Convenant on Economic, Social and Cultural Rights, Leiden et al. 2006, 3, UN Committee on ESC Rights, General Comment No. 9, UN Doc. E/1998/24, Article 10.

[11]Kriele, Martin, Die Menschenrechte zwischen Ost und West, Gütersloh 1977, 16-17.

12

education transcends the sovereign power of the states, and the supranational organisation is not legitimized to act as a supervisor for international conventions or a judge in a trial concerning independent states which refused to sign the contracts of the International Courts. Control is restricted to communication on the same level in order to maintain or achieve the pluralistic balance of the world's nations. Ruling on the ESC rights of bright individuals and their justiciability is restricted to the national constitution which can prescribe measures and regulations in form of soft law determining the competence of arbitrary courts and committees and hard law which should be subject to the national parliament, constitution and laws. The determination of whether or not a treaty provision is self-executing and capable of being applied directly by domestic courts without transformation into national law by the legislative is a matter for the national constitution to determine.

Justiciability basically presupposes the decision of an independent judicial organ pertaining to the right in question. It contains a material element implying that the law is applicable to be legally recoverable and a procedural element designating access to justice in form of a legal recourse for the claim based on the infringement of the right to education as well as legal aid and advice. There is no agreement on whether it is sufficient that only some of the violations are justiciable. Effective legal protection presupposes that the case is dealt with by an independent court in an appropriate period of time and that it is possible for the plaintiff to achieve the objective the legal order aims at.[12]

According to Article 8 of the Universal Declaration of Human Rights, the party subject to the infringement of basic laws has the right to constitutional remedy.

Article 28 of the Convention on the Rights of the Child grants access to higher education based on capacity and Article 29 rules that the education of the child shall be directed to the development of the child's personality, talents and mental and physical abilities to their fullest

---

[12]Franco, Ana Maria Suárez, Die Justiziabilität wirtschaftlicher, sozialer und kultureller Menschenrechte. Eine Untersuchung über den aktuellen Zustand in Lateinamerika, unter Beachtung der völkerrechtlichen Menschenrechtsstandards, in: Studien zum internationalen, europäischen und öffentlichen Recht, ed. by Riedel, Eibe, Vol. 24, Frankfurt am Main et al. 2010, 50-57.

potential. The right to education according to Principle 7 of the Declaration of the Rights of the Child does not refer to merit.

Article 26 of the Universal Declaration of Human Rights does not emphasize the necessity for a nurturing of gifted individuals in special programs.

Article 26 of the Universal Declaration of Human Rights, Everyone has the right to education. (...) and higher education shall be equally accessible to all on the basis of merit.

Article 13 of the International Covenant on Economic, Social and Cultural Rights, which implies that higher education shall be made equally accessible on the basis of capacity, does not breach this rule. Capacity is assessed regarding the expertise and experience of the student.[13] The interpretation of this formulation used in

---

[13]UN Committee on ESC Rights, General Comment No. 13, UN Doc. E/1999/10.

General Comment No. 13 does not restrict the affirmation of capacity to success in examinations, which is arguably a teachable skill.[14]

Article 3 of the Convention against Discrimination in Education permits differences in treatment by the public authorities of nationals based on merit, and Article 4 implies that access to higher education is based on individual capacity.

Article 3 (c) of the Convention against Discrimination in Education, Not to allow any differences of treatment by the public authorities between nationals, except on the basis of merit or need, in the matter of school fees and the grant of scholarships or other forms of assistance to pupils and necessary permits and facilities for the pursuit of studies in foreign countries.

---

[14]Hodgkin, Rachel, Newell, Peter, Implementation Handbook for the Convention on the Rights of the Child, UNICEF, third ed., New York 2007, 425.

16

Regional

According to Article 11 of the African Charter on the Rights and Welfare of the Child, education shall be directed to the promotion and development of the child's personality, talents and mental and physical abilities to their fullest potential. Furthermore, States Parties shall take all appropriate measures to make higher education accessible to all on the basis of capacity and ability, and to take special measures in respect of female, gifted and disadvantaged children. According to Article 17 of the African Charter on Human and Peoples' Rights, ruling on the right to education does not refer to merit.

Article XXI of the Universal Islamic Declaration of Human Rights contains a right to education based on natural capability while Article 41 of the Arab Charter on Human Rights does not take ability into consideration but includes adult education. Lifelong learning should not be restricted to in-service training but should include the acquisition of a professional entry requirement.

Article XII of the American Declaration of the Rights and Duties of Man contains the right to an education including the right to equality of opportunity in every case, in accordance with natural talents and merit. Article

13 of the Additional Protocol to the American Convention on Human Rights in the Area of Economic, Social and Cultural Rights "Protocol of San Salvador" grants access to higher education based on individual capacity.

Article 17 of the European Social Charter grants children and young persons the right to appropriate social, legal and economic protection without reference to their ability. Article 14 of the European Charter of Fundamental Rights and Article 2 of Protocol No. 1 of the European Convention for the Protection of Human Rights and Fundamental Freedoms include a right to education not based on merit.

The Sudan

In contrast to the right to education of Article 44, the general principle of Article 13 of the Constitution of the Sudan of the year 2005 ruling on teaching, science, art and culture does not grant a mandatory right but may be used as an interpretation aid. Article 44 implies a right to participate in education and the person concerned is capable of pursuing a claim based on the violation of the right before the Supreme Court according to Articles 48, 61 and 78. While Article 28 of the Child Act of the Sudan of the year 2009 includes the right to education for the child, Article 30 provides a reward for excellent children in an explicit way.

> Article 30 of the Child Act of the Sudan of the year 2009, Children at schools may be rewarded for academic excellence and cultural and artistic creation, as the regulations made by the Ministry of Instruction and General Education may specify.

Germany

In the German Constitution the right to education is not explicitly ruled but it is derived from other Articles by means of interpretation. Article 11 of the state constitution of Baden Württemberg implies a sponsoring for each young person based on merit. Hans Dieter Jarass regards the general freedom of action according to Article 2 and the general school system pursuant to Article 7 as a legal basis for the right to education.[15] According to the decision of the Federal Constitutional

---

[15]Jarass, Hans Dieter, Zum Grundrecht auf Bildung und Ausbildung, in: Die Öffentliche Verwaltung 1992, 674-679, 678.

Court, the governmental task of providing a school system based on Article 7 of the German Constitution establishing educational opportunities for young citizens in relation to their capacity does not grant a subjective right. [16] Stephan Hobe fundamentally agrees and demands a right of the child to special promotion at school based on merit, as premised in Articles 2 and 3 and the welfare state principle of the German Constitution.[17]

The United States of America

The federal constitution of the United States of America does not imply a right to education. The states can choose to provide this right according to the Fourteenth Amendment based on the equal protection clause. Jacob K. Javits Gifted and Talented Students Education Act does not provide a mandatory right.

---

[16]German Federal Constitutional Court, Decision 59, 360.
[17]Hobe, Stephan, Gibt es ein Grundrecht auf begabungsgerechte Einschulung? Zur Verfassungs-mäßigkeit der Stichtagsregelung des § 42 Abs. 2 des Schulgesetzes Schleswig-Holstein (SchulG SH), in: Die Öffentliche Verwaltung 1996, 190-199, 195-196.

Summary

Although a lot of international and regional treaties and national constitutions determine the right to education, the existence of a legal foundation for a mandatory right to a special sponsoring and schooling of gifted individuals can be denied.

The decision concerning the educational ways chosen to guarantee that the gifted individual is empowered to develop his potential is a matter of interpretation and the principle of equality. Financial and non-material support for the gifted individual can be a positive contribution to an extraordinary achievement if the talented person invests effort in it. But even under moderate circumstances he is often capable of developing an exceptional skill. The successful nurturing of the bright person does not presuppose a pedagogical influence focused on realising the special potential but requires refraining from inhibition of the self-developing individual capacity. The talented person should be enabled to demand equal opportunities and to develop a self-conception based on his existing traits including his giftedness and not on alienation.

As far as merit is concerned as a basis for promotion, it implies that the student shows an expected behaviour considered to prove his advanced learning ability in comparison to other students, taking into account that giftedness is a complex and individual trait and ability is not always measurable within the comparative frame of didactical reduction. Because of the small number of exceptionally skilled individuals and their search for achievements not aligned to a certain scale, the creation of an amendment to the relevant right to education would not contribute to the goal-orientated discovery and effective nurturing of the extraordinary scientists and artists of this century. The gifted individual is entitled to special sponsoring in order to establish equality with the common procedure of promoting students of average condition.

Bibliography

Aunión, Juan Antonio, Los campus pierden el monopolio del saber, El País, 30. 12. 2014, 26-27.

Abd al-Aziz, Amir, Huquq al-insan fi-l-islam, 1997.

Baumann, Zygmunt, Legislators and Interpreters. On Modernity, Post-Modernity and Intellectuals, Cambridge et al. 1995.

Beiter, Klaus Dieter, The Protection of the Right to Education by International Law. Including a Systematic Analysis of Article 13 of the International Convenant on Economic, Social and Cultural Rights, Leiden et al. 2006.

Delbrück, Jost, The Right to Education as an International Human Right, in: German Yearbook of International Law, Vol. 35, 1992, 92-104.

Evered, Lisa J., Jarwan, Fathi A. et al., Jordan's Jubilee School. Educating the Arab World's Gifted Students, in: Gifted Child Today, Vol. 20, 1997, 46-49.

Franco, Ana Maria Suárez, Die Justiziabilität wirtschaftlicher, sozialer und kultureller Menschenrechte. Eine Untersuchung über den aktuellen Zustand in Lateinamerika, unter Beachtung der völkerrechtlichen Menschenrechtsstandards, in: Studien zum internationalen, europäischen und öffentlichen Recht, ed. by Riedel, Eibe, Vol. 24, Frankfurt am Main et al. 2010.

Gardner, Howard, Frames of Mind. The Theory of Multiple Intelligences, New York 2011.

Gardner, Howard, Intelligenzen. Vielfalt des menschlichen Geistes, fourth ed., Stuttgart 2013.

German Federal Constitutional Court, Decision 59, 360.

Gowan, John Curtis, Alienation, in: California Personnel and Guidance Association, Vol. 1, 1968-69, 4-7.

Hobe, Stephan, Gibt es ein Grundrecht auf begabungsgerechte Einschulung? Zur Verfassungs-mäßigkeit der Stichtagsregelung des § 42 Abs. 2 des Schulgesetzes Schleswig-Holstein (SchulG SH), in: Die Öffentliche Verwaltung 1996, 190-199.

Hodgkin, Rachel, Newell, Peter, Implementation Handbook for the Convention on the Rights of the Child, UNICEF, third ed., New York 2007.

Jarass, Hans Dieter, Zum Grundrecht auf Bildung und Ausbildung, in: Die Öffentliche Verwaltung 1992, 674-679.

Karpen, Ulrich, Rechtsfragen des lebenslangen Lernens. Eine vergleichende Untersuchung zum deutschen, französischen, englischen und amerikanischen Verfassungsrecht, in: Recht und Staat in Geschichte und Gegenwart, 490, 491, Tübingen 1979.

Kriele, Martin, Die Menschenrechte zwischen Ost und West, Gütersloh 1977.

Oshana, Marina A. L., Autonomy and Self-Identity, in: Autonomy and the Challenges to Liberalism. New Essays, Cambridge 2008, 77-97.

Raina, M. K., Perspectives on the Gifted and Talented Disadvantaged in India, in: Worldwide Perspectives on the Gifted Disadvantaged, ed. by Wallace, Belle, Adams, Harvey B., Bicester 1993, 304-329.

Schliesky, Utz, Hoffmann, Christian et al., Schutzpflichten und Drittwirkung im Internet. Das Grundgesetz im digitalen Zeitalter, ed. by the Deutschen Institut für Vertrauen und Sicherheit im Internet, Vol. 1, Baden-Baden 2014.

Spahn, Christine, Wenn die Schule versagt. Vom Leidensweg hochbegabter Kinder, Asendorf 1997.

Sternberg, Robert J., Wisdom, Intelligence, and Creativity Synthesized, Cambridge 2007.

UN Committee on ESC Rights, General Comment No. 9, UN Doc. E/1998/24, Article 10.

UN Committee on ESC Rights, General Comment No. 13, UN Doc. E/1999/10.

Verheyde, Mieke, Article 28. The Right to Education. A Commentary on the United Nations Convention on the Rights of the Child, ed. by Alen, André, Vande Lanotte, Johan et al., Leiden et al. 2006.

Zirkel, Perry A., The Case Law on Gifted Education. A New Look, in: Gifted Child Quarterly, Vol. 48, 2004, 309-314.

www.ingramcontent.com/pod-product-compliance
Lightning Source LLC
Chambersburg PA
CBHW061453180526
45170CB00004B/1693